Growing Pains

GROWING PAINS

All rights reserved. No part of this book may be used or reproduced in any manner whatsoever without written permission, except in the context of reviews and critical articles.

edited by: Shelby Leigh

Print ISBN: 978-1-7386322-0-6
Ebook ISBN: 978-1-7386322-1-3

copyright © 2022 by Sierra Madison Brown-Rodrigues

www.sierramadison.com

Table of Contents

Author's Note	7
every night	10
fragmented	11
burn me alive	12
temporary	13
sunshine	14
a woman's love	15
on how i love:	16
you'll always have a seat at my dinner table	18
blind	19
forbidden fruits	21
hungry	22
my chimera	23
liars	24
a question i don't want the answer to	25
he will also break my heart	26
peace is for the ignorant	29
his car is a money pit but god are there some good memories in it	30
i am not a team player	31

this is how i told you i loved you	*32*
fish out of water	*33*
purity is an unfamiliar taste	*34*
i hope you find someone gentler	*35*
96° 48' 35"	*36*
the problem with us	*37*
heartbreaks are becoming too familiar	*38*
there are no winners in a battle of love	*40*
limbo	*41*
a bad lover	*42*
damned from the start	*43*
two different planets	*44*
a poem about love	*45*
mosaic	*49*
to become a woman	*50*
stale bread	*51*
if i bared my soul to you what would you see?	*52*
the moment	*53*
strange behaviour	*54*
i think i like to be watched	*55*
this city is not tainted yet	*56*

Growing Pains

growing pains — *57*

she's a real bitch — *58*

abandonment issues — *59*

how many times do i need to remind you? — *62*

gold-plated trophy — *63*

good writers are born, not made. — *64*

love's embrace — *65*

pity — *67*

life and death (as i understand it) — *68*

my hometown is a distant memory now — *69*

lonely — *70*

who i am — *71*

her — *72*

unhinged — *73*

for all those who have felt the heavy weight of getting older.

Author's Note

Dear Reader,

I am writing this as a 23-year-old woman when these words came bleeding out of me when I was much younger. There is beauty in looking back at all this writing and remembering who I was back then and who I am now. It has been a bittersweet journey, one, dearest reader, that I now offer you a front-row seat to.

I invite you to explore my adolescence, though I must caution that you might find yourself lost along the way. I know I did. To feel the crushing weight of morality is to accept that you are always getting older, and maybe not that much wiser. These words are now yours. I offer them on a silver platter and hope that they fill you up. If they don't, that's fine as well; it's your party, I just catered it.

Growing Pains is a collection of poetry and prose, of me trying to figure out who to love, how to lose, and what it means to become a woman. It came to me during some of the darkest hours, as I sat under the moonlight wondering, *is this it?* It may not always make sense, but it has become fused so deeply with my being that it feels as though I am handing you over a piece of my heart. I just ask you to treat it kindly.

I cannot truly put into words the gratitude I have for you to simply be holding this in your hands. It is not easy to share your soul with the world, so let us keep this just between us, shall we?

If you are struggling with the act of growing up, please remember that growing pains fade and you will always be enough, no matter where you land.

Yours forever,
        Sierra x

i.

digging my own grave

every night

do not light a fire
across my body every night
(with light caresses of your fingertips,
soft murmurs of love,
lips over my stomach,
hands gripping my hips)
and expect me to
put it out every morning.

fragmented

in a city so large
there are still intersections
that did not exist to me
before you: i pass streets
and cannot help to smile
as i remember you tossing me
over your shoulder
while we ran in the rain, leaving pieces
of who we were scattered on the sidewalks.

a whole city
i am forced to remember
in fragments of you.

burn me alive

i am the sun looming
over a daisy field
filling it with sunshine
and warmth; you laid
there for hours soaking
it all in, thinking you deserved it
but now that i am gone, and you are cold
i hope you realise i had
to burn myself just to bring you comfort.

temporary

thank you for teaching me
i am resilient in ways
i never knew possible,
that rock bottom is
only made up of pebbles
i can climb up from
with fingertips dirty and bruised.
water will wash away the pain
but it cannot wash
your lingering touch
from my trembling skin.

ageing has taught the
cruel lesson of fleetingness
and you were the same,
watching idly as i drowned
leaving me stranded with no life boat
even though you knew
i was a terrible swimmer.

sunshine

i keep you alive in pieces
of my lonely heart.
you are a ghost in my attic
haunting, looming, creeping,
over my every movement,
taunting with a crooked smile
and sharp fingers; but it is spring
and the windows are open
creaking in the wind
as sunshine streams in.
i hope it is bright enough
to cast you out.

a woman's love

you pray to a man in the sky
when all you could ever ask for
sits beside you on a cool august evening
with a pleated skirt and gentle eyes.

what is your prayer
to the love of a woman?

on how i love:

knees bruised
legs open
throat hoarse
palms outstretched in a plea
tears like silk gliding down my cheeks.

this is how i love,
this is how i love you.

if i'm to feel the crushing weight of longing, let it be by you, and all our unfinished business.

you'll always have a seat at my dinner table

bittersweetness tangs my tongue
like iron blood pouring into my mouth
after accidentally biting my lip;
i know you must go
like how i know winter must come
if i ever want another summer,
but i can't help the sorrow
that wiggles its way around my lungs.
a forest of potential
budded inside my cavities
and was just as quickly wiped out
by wildfires of deception.

watching you walk away
feels a lot like leaving for college.
my mother was happy i left
but i know she keeps
the door creaked ever so slightly
so i can always find my way home
even if the streetlights are burnt out.

i'll do the same for you;
my door will always
be left a sliver open
in case you ever want to
stop by for coffee.
i know i'm not home, you told me so,
but my dinner table
has a placemat for you
and i still have your favourite mug
(i glued it back together).

blind

i have cried
to the gods so loudly
(pleaded under the
guise of darkness
on bruised knees)
that i am sure i have awoken them
from the deepest of slumbers.
and they sighed,

*stupid girl, don't you know
we only take what was never yours to keep.*

blind to what will soon be gifted,
treasures handcrafted by them
into my palms.

*my heart is buried in you, i never bothered to
ask for it back.*

forbidden fruits

alien fingers skimming
down my rib cage
leaving tingles as hot
as fire across my skin.
this is always how it starts:
letting myself taste forbidden fruits
convincing myself their sourness
will eventually turn sweet.
the bitterness in my mouth
lingers a fraction too long
but i learn to yearn for the taste.

here i go again, making another god
out of a lover with frail bones
and i will cry when they
remind me they're just human.

hungry

i have never been good
at just dipping my toe in
—i cannot love without
letting it consume me;
it must take me by my hair
and drag me across the floor.

i cannot love in small doses
i let myself overdose on it,
let myself fall in love with
people and places and moments
until my stomach no longer
feels the pang of hunger.
but just as quickly as it comes
it fades, forcing me to look for scraps
just to keep myself full.

eventually it becomes time
to do it all again, to rebuild
on the bones of heartache.

my chimaera

your ghost in the distance
teasing me, as if i will ever again
be able to touch you,
or hold you, or call you mine.
the summer looks good on you:
does my touch haunt your freckled skin?
i remain vigilant in the darkest of hours
with you on my mind, i am so full of you
i cannot possibly sleep
(i think i have been up for three days now).

i sit in harrowing pain
each moment of this haunting.
sever you from my skin
my chimaera, oh my chimaera,
your spirit stays here
between the delicate intricacies
of my heart, i couldn't possibly
leave you behind.

liars

lie to me as your lips touch mine
as sweet as honey, hot as the july heat;
wandering hands find refuge on my hips
pulling me closer, closer, closer.

you leave the door open for me
so i can sneak into your house
like something smaller than a mouse,
taking up minimal space
as i walk up your creaky stairs
with white toenails and coffee-stained teeth
hoping i don't wake the neighbours.

in the mornings our limbs are tangled
and your soft snores wake me before
the sun: you taught me you can build
a whole life on lies and it will taste just
as good as the real thing.

a question i don't want the answer to

did you ever look at me and just for a split second want to be better? for me? (as selfish of a request as that may be). did i ever, even once, strike a nerve so deep inside of you that urged you to be a better man? how did you hold me every time i cried and not do better? you said all the right things, stroked all the right places, worshipped me in ways i didn't know i needed. but when push came to shove you had no problem flicking me off that edge. you had no problem watching me fall and break my skull on rocks, staring idly as blood oozed from my wounded flesh. for someone who said they didn't like guts, you had no problem closing your eyes until you felt the glory. were you better for her? i don't think i want the answer.

he will also break my heart

he isn't you. there is no chaos in his life quite like there was in yours. i welcome the silence, nestle myself into arms strong enough to hold all the weight of my fears. where you dropped me he picks me up, and i can't help but look up with babydoll eyes and wonder why i ever fought so hard for you.

*we both knew one of us wouldn't make it out
alive. we dug too deep for someone to not make
a home out of a grave.*

ii.

all is fair in love and war.

peace is for the ignorant

i sit in bed with cold pizza at my feet
watching my cat rise and fall
as he sleeps peacefully, i can't help
but wonder about that type of tranquillity.

i can't wait to see you, he texts me.

ditto, i say.

he tells me to sleep well
as if i can sleep at all
without somebody beside me
to distract me from the fact
that i am never at peace.

his car is a money pit but god are there some good memories in it

moments not caught on tape
life just happening—it keeps moving
despite vacant cries, screams to stop;
all these seconds just passing us by
turning into distant memories
by the time we digest them.

us in the car—swallowing every
nitty gritty burning memory,
i could have vomited up all the hurt and pain
and blood into your lap.
i could not stay walking on eggshells
crying into pillows that never dried.

god the way he holds me
puts your touch to shame;
his hands convince me i am not
as damned as i once thought.
nothing is caught in my mouth
as i sit in his car, we drive and sing along
to songs decades old; there are no
guts to be shed, no hurt to vomit up.
he rests his hand on my thigh
and i start to think i'm falling for him.

i am not a team player

we are playing a dangerous game, you and i. lying here in each other's arms, your hot breath on my neck telling me i am beautiful. we pretend like i have any heart left to give, any love lingering in empty hallows of a worn-out body. he dug me a grave and i am still waiting to climb out. i am sorry. *kiss me,* you say. i will, but please do not forget i am not here to stay—i am always one foot out the door.

this is how i told you i loved you

it is the dead of winter and
your window is open (you like
the room cold and i like you
so i don't tell you i am frozen
to the bone). you caress my skin
with fingers so soft i'm afraid the
hallows of my cheeks will shatter
them; i did not know love could be
so sweet, like caramel cascading down
me (so sweet i can lick it right off
my fingers). before it felt like a game
i had to win but you don't count
the times i fall short, the laps
i slow down on, the scraped knees
and bloody chin, none of it
matters to you, you love me
just because. no games stretched
out across soul-crushing rounds, just
gentle fingertips and morning kisses.

you asked me about love and
the men before you but i'm
not quite sure now that was love,
i think it was just survival.

fish out of water

what does it say about me
that when life is slow and steady
and filled up with laughter
that seeps between the
cracks in my ribs, that i still
long for more? it seems i have
everything i've ever asked for:
have i asked the gods for too little?
have they given me comfort
and apologised when nothing meaningful comes from
it?

*we have given you love and happiness and
mundaneness,* they say,

but signed it with a reminder
that it will never be enough for me,
it will never fill me up completely.
i can either accept this sobering fact
and live between moments, gasping for air
(like a fish out of water) or leave
behind the only good i've ever known.

i love you but i am sorry,
i am too selfish to stay for long.

purity is an unfamiliar taste

you are my purest love, all sweet dripping like honey
down the navel of my stomach, the only bitter we know
in our drinks. my god i have spent years writing poems
in capital letters about LOVE, pretending i had any
indication of what that meant, how that felt. waltzing
between fragments of my past, i am hoping you don't
see how complicated of a dance this is but shouldn't be.
that you do not notice i miss every step, force you back,
step on your toes. purity cannot erase the distaste in my
mouth, and yet here i am rinsing it out again and again
and again, praying i can be pure and sweet and loving.

i hope you find someone gentler

whenever i am in love
i forget who i am: the core
of my being gets coated in syrup
and the fight that ignites me
swiftly fizzles out. i suddenly
become satisfied with goodnight
kisses and afternoon cuddles,
exposing my underbelly in hopes of
gentle affection. my veins crave
the adventure of heartbreak, the
never-ending feeling of waiting
for something new, someone new.

i love you, in whatever
wicked way i can;
do not think i don't,
i just crave something more.

96° 48' 35"

we signed our names at the centre
of the country, long before we felt love;
before we settled into lives that no
longer felt like our own cradling our
relationship as if its fragility was assumed.
is that where we went wrong?
slapping a label on the side of the box before
ever opening it up, as if a few bumps
in the car could break it? (that we could peek
inside when we got home and see no
resemblance of anything whole).

there is a part of my stomach
that aches at our naivety, that
still remembers the younger versions
of ourselves giggling on road trips
and in the bathtubs of 3-star hotels.

we exist, somewhere on that sign
and one day another young couple
will sign their names over ours
and that will be the final nail in the coffin.

the problem with us

was that you wanted me
to be someone different,
someone holy and foreign
that whispered prayers to you
under the stars. my appetite
was too big you said, i ought
to be reminded that girls like me
don't always get what we want
that i should be grateful for your love
in all its fleetingness.

the problem with us
is that you opened the door
teasing me to leave, telling me
there is no universe where a girl like me
finds someone half as good as you.
i've always had a problem with
spite, that may be a curse of my own
but once you opened that door
i was gone, running down the street
never looking back.

i heard from a friend of
a friend that you asked about me
a few months later, that i felt
more like an enigma
to you than an ex-lover.

i like it that way.

heartbreaks are becoming too familiar

i am young, learning that heartbreaks are the one part of life i don't think i will ever master. every time, i sacrifice parts of myself to try to fit into moulds that weren't designed for me. after it all, i am left to fall into my own arms, left to wonder if our promises lay limp in the air, if we carry everything we started but never finished in an oversized backpack. onto the next.

*the love was there.
i saw it, i felt it, it was real.*

there are no winners in a battle of love

and there it was—the unwavering truth to the end. a battlefield with no winner, just collateral on both sides. the strange foreign feeling of being encapsulated in arms that no longer feel like home but rather somewhere nostalgic. a bittersweet goodbye with half-smiles and quivering hands returning hoodies and socks. it hurt more to look back and not pinpoint where we went wrong—what path led us so astray that i no longer see the sparkle of love in your eye. it's been replaced by a shimmer of knowingness, of *i am so glad you were in my life but the door is open and i must ask you to leave.* all i can say is, *thank you for letting me stop by.*

limbo

i guess i'll sit here and watch you
on my friend activity tab
beaming from my blue lit screen
in the middle of the night, as if
some sad songs could equate
to the earthquake of our heartache.

goodbyes are harder when
i can watch you from afar;
my dear i am sorry our love
story came to a screeching halt,
i promise i wrote hundreds of
love letters to you in red ink
and signed them with my
unfaltering affection. please
do not think my love simply
disappeared, it is stuck in limbo
somewhere looking for someplace
to call home, and i'm hoping,
maybe just this once,
it settles in the den of my bones.

a bad lover

i am a lover who does not
know how to love: it pours
out at all the wrong times
in all the wrong ways.
leaving cups half empty, half full.
when i love too much they leave
when i love too little it's all on me,
where is the line? is it even visible?

i have sat in my room writing poetry
(full of run-on sentences trying to
escape your love) and all i can do is
write, and take too-hot showers that
leave my skin red. maybe if i had shown
you these burning words you
would have understood.

i am at the funeral wearing all black
watching you fake a smile. i made treats
and brought wine and even told you
you're right. i am mourning at a wake that
i never had to think about wondering
where we went wrong.
do i mourn for you or for me or for us
(do we even exist in an us)?
heartbreak doesn't feel
like i remember it it hits
deeper, harder, filling weak bones
with poison that speeds up self-hatred.

where does all the love go when
there are no more cups to fill?
where do all the bad lovers end up?

damned from the start

i spent a lot of my childhood
sitting in lawyer's offices
and police stations
as my parents fought to
never have to see each other again
and i was taught that
to love is to constantly be at
war, even in the end.

part of me will always think
i am on a battlefield,
it was bred into my DNA
that there is always a
battle to be won, a fight to
come out victorious from.
sometimes i wonder if
any of it made a difference;
i think i was damned from the start.
there was no other way for me to be:
i was birthed while the moon
was in chaos and i will die when
the stars combust.

i might have been a child back then
but i am still a little girl that doesn't
know better, who is always at war with herself.

two different planets

i. when you held me in your arms for the first time, you held on so tight (too tight), as if i would just slip through your fingers if you eased up. i told you i am not a quiet little thing that could vanish, i am big and loud and chaotic, i could not go anywhere delicately. you smiled, telling me that is the best part about me: i am hard to ignore. months later you avoid my gaze at parties as if my voice does not register in your world any longer.

ii. at supper, we sit across from each other, you are cutting your steak wrong, and i correct you; we bicker like my parents did before i had two homes. i realized then we are very different, too different to ever figure it out. it is like we were born on separate planets and there will always be distance between us. distance not even the stars could shrink. you claim the French are forthright, and i am too sensitive to ever be a writer in Paris, your words are laced with so much venom i am almost impressed. we don't last much longer, and i quickly forget what your arms feel like. sometime after i have supper with another man, a few years older than you, and he cuts his steak properly and reads the books i suggest to him. he isn't much, but he's enough to convince me that i won't have to venture across planets for every lover i have.

a poem about love

i want to write a poem about love, or maybe about the loss of it. i tell myself it will be sweet and pure, like honey dripping down my chin on a midsummer's night, while we sit on your father's back porch and watch the sunset. i want to write about the feeling, *that* feeling, when they tell you they love you for the first time. the way your heart heats up as hot as the sun and beats in your chest as if to whisper, i am home. i have made a home out of you. maybe i will write about how the world seems to get a bit brighter, and feel a little warmer when you're in love's embrace. i am not a fool—i know i had a life before love, and cruelly, i will have one after it, but that does not stop me from wanting to exist only within. i want to write a poem about love even though i have spent the last couple weeks a little bit less myself because of it. even though the world is back to being a fraction duller, and a little bit colder. i want to write about love pretending like it doesn't leave you gasping for air on quiet little side streets, listening to Christmas music sail over from neighbouring cafes. pretend like it doesn't turn nice boys into grim reapers, collecting the soul of who you were while you were with them. maybe i should tell you how it is. that it is not always as sweet as honey. that you'll never return to that back porch and watch the sunset in their arms. as sad as that fact is, you'll always have the memory of it. it is easier to lie to myself about love than it is to lie to the world. they say the poets know best, that they break their own hearts for art but i would have stopped writing all together if you told me the love would stick around forever. maybe that is the part of love that you cannot outrun, no matter if you are a veteran or not. you cannot escape the way it consumes you, the way it fills you up until you look in the mirror and wonder who is looking back at you.

i want to write a poem about love, and i am sure that one day i will, because if there is one lesson i have learned, it is that it never truly fades away. the sun stills sets on that back porch. we are just no longer there to watch it.

*one day i hope you can forgive me for not being
who you thought i was.*

iii.

becoming a woman, in all of her glory.

mosaic

i am a mosaic made up of former lovers and fumbled friendships. there are songs i listen to that transport me back to moments already lived—moments that remind me of the illusion of myself. the hollows of my body do not belong to me; i love things because someone else loved them first. the way i laugh and cry and kiss and fuck was taught, not given. i am constantly being thrown the scraps of other people's lives and calling it my existence.

to become a woman

it is the getting older that is killing me—the watching people who had a reserved seat at my dinner table leave without so much as a whisper, the not recognizing myself in the mirror, the figuring out how to deal with grief in a way that is not all-consuming. inevitably, the getting older happens, the heartbreak and the heartache, the changing, the mourning of those moved on. the hardest part may be realising it is now time to grow into a woman, and in order to do so i must shed the skin of the young girl, for she can only bring me so far. i have spent years writing love letters to boys who leave them in their mailboxes to rot and collect dust. i have forgotten to send sonnets to the girl who carried me through it all. giving up the girl, the doe-eyed innocent lover, in exchange for the woman. what a hard goodbye, to only now acknowledge the heavy weight she carried to let me get to this point. yes, i think the hardest part of growing up is realising the only way to make space for the woman is to let the girl go, and thank her for getting me this far.

stale bread

i worry that if i'm not
completely obsessed
(filled up to the brim)
with someone, suddenly
all my writing will taste stale
like weeks-old bread left
out on the counter by accident.

if i bared my soul to you what would you see?

i am afraid there is nothing
good inside, that i am made
up of everybody else
i've ever known, ever loved.
like a sponge i've absorbed
the best parts of people,
taking their finest attitudes
and wearing it like a scarf.

what is my own soul
if not a mirror of it all, of
everyone and everything
i have deemed good enough?
if you peeled away my skin
like an orange what would be left?

pull away my flesh only to
be face-to-face with the truth;
sinful blood fills my veins,
metaphors scramble my brains,
there are no flowers blooming
in my lungs, i water dead leaves
hoping for the birth of something
that doesn't resemble me.

the moment

last night, sitting with a glass of rosé on the porch of my college house (as fog rolled through the street and fireworks crackled like gunshots all around me), i finally knew what they meant when they said falling in love with yourself was the best part.

strange behaviour

foreign fingers nestled in my hair
and inside me, my friends tell me
this is the best part of being single
(i don't know if i agree). we kiss
as if you know my middle name
or the street i grew up on; in the morning
we sit over coffee wearing shy smiles
and i am overbearing, bombarding you
with questions and you answer
without a grimace, without skipping a beat like
you too hope to know enough about me
that i don't feel like a stranger.
i know you don't like me in the
way the others have but you seem
nice and sweet and you taste like
strawberries in the summer.

i am not broken but your chairs are creaky
and this coffee reminds me of him.
we are dancing on the line of a
friendly affair yet i will not ask for
a ceasefire, you feel too good in
the limelight and your body reminds
me i am human; but it is strange,
so very very strange, to know what
you taste like but not know your middle name.

i think i like to be watched

i am watching my cat
eat his dinner,
so small and frail
and his life completely
up to me. something
about this moment
feels innately human
as i lean against the
cold wall, its bareness
resting in between
my shoulder blades.

i look like how i would
if someone else was
watching me: sorta all wrong
and trying to be someone
outside myself.

i wonder what i would
look like if i truly thought
no one was watching.

this city is not tainted yet

every time i start to hate the city i live in, i walk down the street at 1 in the morning to the corner store that sells overpriced frozen pizza and packaged deviled eggs, and a bus drives past, route 26, and i am right back where i was when i fell in love with it all. i am 18, moving into an apartment without my mom and this city is full of new beginnings. now i am holding onto words and people and places and all of it is blurry, as if the lights of this city have finally blinded me.

growing pains

i am 13, all limbs
standing on bambi legs,
always wobbling, never stable.
frail bones hold me up; i feel like
i can almost touch the sky.
my mother watches movies with me
every friday night and i'm still small enough
to fit into the cupboard under the sink.

i am 23 and my limbs ache
from running and crashing
and drowning under the weight
of it all. i am so full of other people
that i'm no longer hungry.
i feel the heaviness of mortality
and what it means to be a woman,
to lay your own body down
in the early hours of the morning
for someone else to hold,
to love and be loved and
then forgotten.

i am 23 and i am all limbs
and empty promises and hope
and fear and longing.

she's a real bitch

i am getting colder again,
and my scalp feels less heavy
(the hair piles in the sink and
my shorts from the 11th grade
fit again). what is the point of
recovery if relapse is inevitable?
i can see the bruises i once
welcomed with a smile,
now they lie on my body as a
painful reminder that
you cannot outrun yourself;
you can stumble down winding roads
of open arms and i love yous
but at the end of the day
she will always be there to meet you.
to whisper in your ear cruel nothings,
of how maybe, just maybe, if you were
smaller, weaker, taking up less space,
maybe then they would have stayed.
she wills you to wither
under her grasp, her face
once appeared slim
and beautiful—now it's brutal
and sharp, her jawline cutting
into every inch of your skin.
it is hard to bloom where
your roots have forced you to stay.

abandonment issues

pretty little girl,
who pretends as though
the world halts when
her eyes are closed.
door open, eyes closed.
you are still at home
you did not leave the
pretty little girl who had
nothing else to offer but her love.
there is no leaving if
you never shut the door,
just a hollow feeling of emptiness
but no, if i do not close the door
it's like you never left.
the pretty little girl
who sat on the side of the road waiting
for strong hands to hold her.
the sidewalk got cold and
she got not so little.
i think of that pretty little girl
all doe-eyed and living in
a fantasy realm
pretending like you never left.
there's no pinpoint of when
the bubble popped, when the
little girl got old and cold
and cynical. still pretty, batting eyes
at strong hands and always leaving
doors open, never closed.
please do not close the door
in my face the slamming
echoes sound like a bomb
ringing in my ears.

i may have silenced it out
but that pretty little girl
doesn't know reality yet.
she stays pretending, deep inside
somewhere even i will not explore.
but she can hear every creaking
footstep so please do not
close the door,
if the door is not closed
maybe it's like you never left.

i have become the woman of my dreams, but at what cost?

how many times do i need to remind you?

i told you from the beginning
that i was not pure or sweet
or something to be treasured;
the way i was meant to be consumed
was in doses and not all together.

do not savour the taste of me,
i am a killer: from the inside out
i will rip you apart. you choose to
break your healthy distance
and wake up with your fingers
tangled in my hair. do not look
at me like i lied when all i ever
did was warn you.

gold-plated trophy

i carry the heartbreak of a daughter
left to harden into a statue of
my own insecurities;
a parade of beautiful women
constantly flaunted
(i do not learn their names
or remember their faces—all i know
is they are taller and prettier than me).
i am a trophy, sitting shiny and new
on the top of the staircase;
i was made to be ogled then discarded
you cannot wield me
into anything else.

good writers are born, not made.

you asked me how to
become a good writer,
how i found my way with words.
i do not tell you that i fumbled
with the hardness of living
as a small child, that i had no
choice but to write to deal with
the heaviness of it all.

instead i say it is something
you are born with, that all
the good writers have a deep
desire for immortality
and the only way we know how to
achieve it is through words.

it is not a lie, but it is also
not my truth.

love's embrace

i am a fool for falling in love
as much as i do, for closing my eyes
and hoping for the best, entering
every moment with the
worst outcome teasing me
like talons scratching
the back of my head whispering
sweet cruelties; it is a voice
that knows me better than
i maybe know myself.

it doesn't let me think about the
innocence of love, not when every
lover has left me bloody, bruised,
shattered. i am beginning to think
i am addicted to endings,
to the rebirth of something
entirely unknown, as if my foundation
of self was always built on the
bones of chaos.

give me love's embrace
and i will make a home out of it.

i don't stand a chance against you. you could ask for my heart on a platter and i would rip it out with my own hands. even after all this time.

pity

i have pity for all the wicked creatures who stir in the night, meaning i have pity for myself—maybe too much—but i am a night owl who weaves her way through the darkness like a young doe who has just lost her mother. i am always on the run from boys with pretty eyes and girls with soft palms. all of it is pitiful: the falling in love, the breaking of bones, the anticipated pain of seeing the sun rise up and knowing that i am not half the person in the daylight that i am under the kiss of midnight.

life and death (as i understand it)

Life sits on the same park bench as Death, twiddling her thumbs as he grins sheepishly. it is not a romantic affair, rather a friendship that bloomed during the most confusing of times. often Life is so wrapped up in other people that she forgets Death is always lingering, talons stroking her back, an ever-present hot breath on her neck. they do not play games, not anymore. Life has a problem with letting go. she holds onto people and places and things a little longer than she must, but Death understands. he is soft and gracious and holds her as she cries when it is time for her to hand someone over. Death reminds her that he does not take them far: he lets them play as butterflies landing on children's noses, allows them to embody the sunlight on a warm summer's day, and he always makes sure that when their loved ones call for them, they answer back, in tiny gestures and evocative air. they sit on that same park bench, always close enough to feel, but never close enough to touch.

my hometown is a distant memory now

i want to be seventeen again, running through the backroads of my hometown, laughter bubbling up from the deepest part of me. a laughter that only comes from someone who hasn't yet broken their seal of innocence, who does not know the harshness of the world she is about to enter. all scraped knees and half-empty liquor bottles hidden between folds of clothes, sneaking out of creaky windows and kissing boys a little too old for her. there are moments sometimes when i feel seventeen again—moments when i can hear the echo of that laugh in myself, bubbling up to my lips but never escaping my mouth. as if i am just missing something, forever perfectly positioned on the cusp of happiness. but i'm an adult now, so i guess i'll have to just settle for artificial moments that taste like the real thing.

lonely

when loneliness hits, it is not a short storm. it is a thunderbolt that ripples through every cell of my being, begging for escape.

begging—like a pitiful little thing—for a second of breath as i watch my body drown.

–there is no worse war than one waged inside your own heart.

who i am

sit with me and i will tell you about who i was before
you. how i was never sure of anything so i spent my
childhood at war with myself, and how my mother's
ageing is an ever-present stake in my heart. i will tell
you about how despite growing up the same, my
brother and i are so very different. let me speak about
when the world ripped apart and i fell through the
cracks and i never really figured out how to get back up
to the surface.

her

i am tired of feeling
like i must always be soft;
i get surprised when people
see the hardness that calluses
my body and choose to caress
me anyways. i know i am beautiful
and sweet and kind but i am
not always those things
and most definitely not all at once
— do you love me or *her*?

her: who dresses in short skirts,
bending over counters with a wink.

her: who nestles her body into your arms while
watching a movie, looking up with submissive eyes.

her: who always knows what to say
and says it with confidence.

one would say i am both me and *her*, that our entities
are intertwined, but sometimes i feel so far away from
her that i wonder if she's a separate person all together.

unhinged

assigned loneliness at birth: it is weaved into my dna. i was born with an affliction for loss built in. i keep tiny notebooks full of absentminded thoughts, constantly jotting down everything i have ever felt as if to understand it all better. but you can't change your blood—you can just cut your flesh open and bleed out.

About the Author

Sierra Madison is a writer born and raised in an unmemorable town that she spent most of her adolescence over-romanticizing. After graduating from the University of Toronto, Sierra has pursued multiple avenues of creative endeavours, however she always finds her way home to pen and paper. Sierra now lives in Toronto with her feline companion Totoro, surrounded by friends and family, spending most of her days writing, reading on over-crowded buses, collecting candles, and drinking extra dirty martinis in hotel bars.

Visit Sierramadison.com

www.ingramcontent.com/pod-product-compliance
Lightning Source LLC
Chambersburg PA
CBHW070331120526
44590CB00017B/2852